step by step

thai

p

This is a Parragon Book
First published in 2002

Parragon
Queen Street House
4 Queen Street
Bath BA1 1HE, UK

ISBN: 0-75258-009-4

Printed in Spain

Produced by The Bridgewater Book Company Ltd, Lewes, East Sussex

Creative Director Terry Jeavons
Art Director Sarah Howerd
Editorial Director Fiona Biggs
Senior Editor Mark Truman
Editorial Assistants Simon Bailey, Tom Kitch
Page Make-up Sara Kidd

NOTES FOR THE READER

- This book uses both metric and imperial measurements. Follow the same units of
  measurement throughout; do not mix metric and imperial measurements.
- All spoon measurements are level: teaspoons are assumed to be 5 ml, and tablespoons are assumed to be 15 ml.
- Unless otherwise stated, milk is assumed to be full-fat, eggs and individual
  vegetables such as potatoes are medium-sized, and pepper is freshly ground
  black pepper.
- Recipes using raw or very lightly cooked eggs should be avoided by infants, the
  elderly, pregnant women, convalescents, and anyone suffering from an illness.
- Optional ingredients, variations, and serving suggestions have not been included
  in the calculations.
- The times given are an approximate guide only. Preparation times differ according
  to the techniques used by different people and the cooking times vary as a result
  of the type of oven used.

Contents

Introduction

Trends in different cultural cuisines from around the world come
and go according to the mood of the moment, but one style of
cookery that is enjoying a lasting popularity is Thai. Food is
serious business to the people of Thailand, and this is reflected
in the wonderful variety of their dishes. The Thai diet revolves
around two main staples – rice, and fish, from the seas that
surround much of the country. Meat dishes are more likely to be
served on special occasions. Fresh, vibrant vegetables, bought
daily from the street markets, add colour and texture. Yet the
real fire and excitement of a Thai dish comes from a handful of
key ingredients – chillies, ginger, garlic and coriander, often
included all together in one recipe. They appear in soups and
sauces, fish cakes and curries, salads and stir-fries, along with
some other classics – lemon grass, limes and coconut milk.

Not only do Thai dishes look and taste sensational but they are
also very easy to prepare and cook. Once the ingredients have

guide to recipe key	
easy	Recipes are graded as follows: 1 pea = easy; 2 peas = very easy; 3 peas = extremely easy.
serves 4	Recipes generally serve four people. Halve the ingredients to serve two, taking care not to mix imperial and metric measurements.
15 minutes	Preparation time. Where recipes include marinating, infusing, soaking or standing, these times are separately noted: eg., 15 minutes, plus 30 minutes to marinate.
15 minutes	Cooking time. Cooking times do not include the cooking of rice or noodles served with the main dishes.

been sliced or chopped, and any sauces prepared, it is often only minutes before the finished dish is ready to serve, so Thai cuisine is ideal for busy cooks. For fast-food addicts, Thai-style Burgers have a kick that is always lacking in the frozen variety, and curry lovers will be intrigued by the Thai Green Fish Curry.

This book offers many ideas for Thai dishes to serve to guests. Chilled Avocado, Lime & Coriander Soup followed by Thai-spiced Coriander Chicken or Spiced Tuna in Sweet-and-Sour Sauce, with a dessert of Steamed Coconut Cake with Lime & Ginger Syrup make an impressive lunch or dinner menu.

Lemon Grass Chicken Skewers, page 74

Soups & Snacks

Thai soups and appetizers or snacks have style and character. Mushrooms and prawns in stock, topped with a garnish of spring onions, gives Thai Fish Soup an appetizing appearance, and fiery red and green chillies make it a taste experience. For a typical Thai snack, try Thai Fish Cakes with Sweet & Sour Dipping Sauce. These are also a treat to linger over at the beginning of a meal. This section includes a version of the most popular Southeast Asian appetizer: Prawn Satay.

Chicken & Coconut Soup

INGREDIENTS

1.2 litres/2 pints chicken
   stock
200 g/7 oz skinless
   boned chicken
1 fresh chilli, split
   lengthways and
   deseeded
7.5 cm/3 inch piece
   lemon grass, split
   lengthways
3 or 4 lime leaves
2.5 cm/1 inch piece fresh
   ginger root, peeled
   and sliced
120 ml/4 fl oz coconut
   milk
6–8 spring onions, sliced
   on the diagonal
¼ tsp chilli purée,
   or to taste
salt
fresh coriander leaves,
   to garnish

❶ Put the stock in a pan with the chicken, chilli, lemon grass, lime leaves and ginger. Bring almost to the boil, reduce the heat, cover, and simmer for 20–25 minutes, or until the chicken is cooked through and firm to the touch.

❷ Remove the chicken and strain the stock. When the chicken is cool, slice thinly or shred into bite-sized pieces.

❸ Return the stock to the saucepan and heat to simmering. Stir in the coconut milk and spring onions. Add the chicken and continue simmering for about 10 minutes, until the soup is heated through and the flavours have mingled.

❹ Stir in the chilli purée. Season to taste with salt and, if wished, add a little more chilli purée.

❺ Ladle the soup into warm bowls and float a few fresh coriander leaves on the surface of the soup as a decoration before serving it.

very easy

serves 4

15 minutes

40–45 minutes

Fish Soup

INGREDIENTS

450 ml/16 fl oz light
   chicken stock
2 lime leaves, chopped
5 cm/2 inch piece lemon
   grass, chopped
3 tbsp lemon juice
3 tbsp Thai fish sauce
2 small, hot green
   chillies, deseeded and
   chopped finely
½ tsp sugar
8 small shiitake
   mushrooms or 8 straw
   mushrooms, halved
1 lb raw prawns, peeled
   if necessary and
   deveined
spring onions, to garnish

TOM YAM SAUCE
4 tbsp vegetable oil
5 garlic cloves, chopped
   finely
1 large shallot, chopped
   finely
2 large hot dried red
   chillies, chopped
   coarsely
1 tbsp dried prawns
   (optional)
1 tbsp Thai fish sauce
2 tsp sugar

❶ First make the tom yam sauce. Heat the oil in a small frying pan and add the garlic. Cook for a few seconds until the garlic just browns. Remove with a slotted spoon and set aside. Add the shallot to the same oil, and fry until browned and crisp. Remove with a slotted spoon and set aside. Add the chillies and fry until they darken. Remove from the oil and drain on kitchen paper. Remove from heat, reserving the oil.

❷ In a small food processor or a spice grinder, grind the dried prawns, if using, then add the reserved chillies, garlic and shallots. Grind to a smooth paste. Return the pan with the original oil to a low heat, add the paste, and warm. Add the fish sauce and sugar, and mix. Remove from the heat.

❸ In a large saucepan, heat the stock and 2 tablespoons of the tom yam sauce. Add the lime leaves, lemon grass, lemon juice, fish sauce, chillies and sugar. Simmer for 2 minutes.

❹ Add the mushrooms and prawns, and cook for an additional 2–3 minutes until the prawns are cooked. Ladle into warm bowls and serve immediately, garnished with the spring onions.

very easy

serves 4

25 minutes

20 minutes

Chicken & Noodle Soup

INGREDIENTS

*1 sheet of dried egg
noodles from a
250 g/9 oz pack*
1 tbsp oil
*4 skinless, boneless
chicken thighs, diced*
*1 bunch spring onions,
sliced*
2 garlic cloves, chopped
*2 cm/ ¾ inch piece fresh
ginger root, chopped
finely*
*850 ml/1½ pints
chicken stock*
*200 ml/7 fl oz
coconut milk*
3 tsp red Thai curry paste
3 tbsp peanut butter
2 tbsp light soy sauce
*1 small red pepper,
chopped*
60 g/2 oz frozen peas
salt and pepper

❶ Put the noodles in a shallow dish and soak in boiling water following the instructions on the packet.

❷ Heat the oil in a large saucepan or a wok, add the chicken, and fry for 5 minutes, stirring until lightly browned. Add the white part of the spring onions, the garlic and ginger, and continue to fry for 2 minutes, stirring.

❸ Add the stock, coconut milk, curry paste, peanut butter and soy sauce, and season to taste. Bring to the boil, stirring, then simmer for 8 minutes, stirring occasionally. Add the red pepper, peas and green spring onion tops, and cook for 2 minutes.

❹ Add the drained noodles and heat through. Spoon into individual bowls and serve with a spoon and a fork.

 very easy

serves 4–6

10 minutes,
plus 5 minutes
to soak

25 minutes

Mushroom & Tofu Broth

INGREDIENTS

4 dried black mushrooms
1 tbsp sunflower oil
1 tsp sesame oil
1 garlic clove, crushed
1 green chilli, deseeded
   and chopped finely
6 spring onions, sliced
1 litre/1¾ pints rich
   brown stock
85 g/3 oz fresh oyster
   mushrooms, sliced
2 kaffir lime leaves,
   shredded finely
2 tbsp lime juice
1 tbsp rice vinegar
1 tbsp Thai fish sauce
85 g/3 oz firm tofu, diced
salt and pepper

 extremely easy

 serves 4

10 minutes,
plus 30 minutes
to soak

10–15 minutes

❶ Pour 150 ml/5 fl oz boiling water over the dried black mushrooms in a heatproof bowl and leave to soak for about 30 minutes. Drain, reserving the liquid, then chop the black mushrooms coarsely.

❷ Heat the sunflower and sesame oils in a large pan or a wok over a high heat. Add the garlic, chilli and spring onions, and stir for 1 minute until softened but not browned.

❸ Add all of the mushrooms, kaffir lime leaves, stock and reserved mushroom liquid. Bring to the boil.

❹ Stir in the lime juice, rice vinegar and fish sauce, lower the heat, and simmer gently for 3–4 minutes.

❺ Add the diced tofu and adjust the seasoning to taste with salt and pepper. Heat gently until boiling, then serve the broth immediately.

COOK'S TIP

Use homemade beef stock, or a Japanese dashi, to make an attractive clear broth. Stock cubes generally make cloudy stock. For a vegetarian version, use vegetable stock and light soy sauce instead of fish sauce.

Chilled Avocado, Lime & Coriander Soup

INGREDIENTS

2 ripe avocados
1 small mild onion,
    chopped
1 garlic clove, crushed
2 tbsp fresh coriander,
    chopped
1 tbsp fresh mint,
    chopped
2 tbsp lime juice
700 ml/1¼ pints
    vegetable stock
1 tbsp rice vinegar
1 tbsp light soy sauce
salt and pepper

GARNISH

2 tbsp soured cream or
    crème fraîche
1 tbsp fresh coriander,
    chopped finely
2 tsp lime juice
lime rind, shredded
    finely

❶ Halve, stone, and scoop out the flesh from the avocados. Place in a blender or a food processor with the onion, garlic, coriander, mint, lime juice and about half the stock, and process until completely smooth.

❷ Add the remaining stock, rice vinegar and soy sauce, and blend again to mix well. Taste and adjust seasoning if necessary with salt and pepper, or with a little extra lime juice if required. Cover the soup with clingfilm, and chill in the refrigerator until needed.

❸ To make the lime and coriander cream garnish, mix together the soured cream, coriander and lime juice. Spoon the mixture into the soup just before serving, and sprinkle with lime rind.

extremely easy

serves 4

10–15 minutes,
plus 2 hours
to chill

0 minutes

Prawn Satay

INGREDIENTS

12 raw king prawns,
 peeled

MARINADE
1 tsp ground coriander
1 tsp ground cumin
2 tbsp light soy sauce
4 tbsp vegetable oil
1 tbsp curry powder
1 tbsp ground turmeric
125 ml/4 fl oz coconut
 milk
3 tbsp sugar

PEANUT SAUCE
2 tbsp vegetable oil
3 garlic cloves, crushed
1 tbsp red curry paste
 (see Red Prawn Curry,
 page 44)
125 ml/4 fl oz coconut
 milk
225 ml/8 fl oz fish or
 chicken stock
1 tbsp sugar
1 tsp salt
1 tbsp lemon juice
4 tbsp unsalted roasted
 peanuts, chopped
 finely
4 tbsp dried
 breadcrumbs

❶ Slit the prawns down their backs and remove the black vein, if any. Set aside. Mix together the marinade ingredients and add the prawns. Mix together well, cover, and set aside for at least 8 hours, or overnight.

❷ To make the peanut sauce, heat the oil in a large frying pan until very hot. Add the garlic and fry until it just starts to colour. Add the curry paste and mix together well, cooking for an additional 30 seconds. Add the coconut milk, stock, sugar, salt and lemon juice, and stir well. Boil for 1 or 2 minutes, stirring constantly. Add the peanuts and breadcrumbs, and mix together well. Pour the sauce into a bowl and set aside.

❸ Using 4 skewers, thread 3 prawns onto each. Cook under a preheated hot grill or on the barbecue for 3–4 minutes on each side until just cooked through. Serve immediately with the peanut sauce.

 very easy

serves 4

15 minutes,
plus 8 hours
to marinate

15–20 minutes

Thai Fish Cakes with Sweet & Sour Chilli Dipping Sauce

INGREDIENTS

450 g/1 lb firm white
  fish, such as hake,
  haddock, or cod,
  skinned and chopped
  coarsely
1 tbsp Thai fish sauce
1 tbsp red curry paste
  (see Red Prawn Curry,
  page 44)
1 kaffir lime leaf,
  shredded finely
2 tbsp chopped
  coriander
1 egg
1 tsp brown sugar
large pinch salt
40 g/1½ oz French
  beans, thinly sliced
  crossways
vegetable oil, for
  shallow-frying

SWEET & SOUR
DIPPING SAUCE
4 tbsp sugar
1 tbsp cold water
3 tbsp white rice vinegar
2 small, hot chillies,
  chopped finely
1 tbsp fish sauce

❶ To make the fish cakes, put the fish, fish sauce, curry paste, lime leaf, coriander, egg, sugar and salt into the bowl of a food processor. Process until smooth. Scrape into a bowl and stir in the French beans. Set aside.

❷ To make the dipping sauce, put the sugar, water and rice vinegar into a small saucepan and heat gently until the sugar has dissolved. Bring to a boil and simmer for 2 minutes. Remove from the heat, stir in the chillies and fish sauce, and leave to cool.

❸ Heat a frying pan with enough oil to cover the bottom generously. Divide the fish mixture into 16 little balls. Flatten the balls into patties and fry them in the hot oil for 1–2 minutes each side until they are golden. Drain on kitchen paper. Serve hot with the dipping sauce.

very easy

serves 4

15 minutes

10 minutes

Prawn & Chicken Sesame Toasts

INGREDIENTS

4 boneless, skinless
   chicken thighs
100 g / 3½ oz cooked
   peeled prawns
1 small egg, beaten
3 spring onions,
   chopped finely
2 garlic cloves, crushed
2 tbsp fresh coriander,
   chopped
1 tbsp Thai fish sauce
½ tsp black pepper
¼ tsp salt
12 slices white bread,
   crusts removed
75 g / 2¾ oz sesame seeds
sunflower oil for shallow
   frying
shredded spring onion
   curls, to garnish

❶ Place the chicken and prawns in a food processor and process until they are chopped very finely. Add the egg, spring onions, garlic, coriander, fish sauce, pepper and salt, and pulse for a few seconds to mix well. Transfer to a bowl.

❷ Spread the mixture evenly over the slices of bread, right to the edges. Scatter the sesame seeds over a plate and press the spread side of each slice of bread into them to coat them evenly.

❸ Using a sharp knife, cut the bread into small rectangles, making 6 per slice.

❹ Pour a 1 cm/½ inch depth of oil into a wide frying pan, and heat it until it is very hot. Fry the bread rectangles quickly in batches for 2–3 minutes until they are golden brown, turning them over once.

❺ Drain the sesame toasts well on kitchen towels and serve hot, garnished with spring onion curls.

extremely easy

serves 4–6

10–15 minutes

5 minutes

Main
Meals

Thai cooking makes use of some delicious marinades which can elevate a basic fish or meat dish. Duck Breasts with Chilli & Lime uses plum jam in a marinade which makes an unusual sticky sauce to drizzle over the grilled meat. In Thai-spiced Salmon, salmon fillets are given a coating of fresh ginger, chilli, lime and sesame oil, with crushed coriander seeds added for still more flavour. These pages include versions of the classic green and red Thai curries with fish and with meat, which are quick and easy to make, and a Thai stir-fry, combining chicken and mango.

Beef & Peppers with Lemon Grass

INGREDIENTS

500 g/1 lb 2 oz lean
  beef fillet
2 tbsp vegetable oil
1 garlic clove,
  chopped finely
1 lemon grass stalk,
  shredded finely
2.5 cm/1 inch piece fresh
  ginger root,
  chopped finely
1 red pepper, deseeded
  and sliced thickly
1 green pepper,
  deseeded and
  sliced thickly
1 onion, sliced thickly
2 tbsp lime juice
boiled noodles or rice,
  to serve

extremely easy

serves 4

10 minutes

10 minutes

❶ Cut the beef into long, thin strips, cutting across the grain.

❷ Heat the oil in a large frying pan or a wok over a high heat. Add the garlic and stir-fry for 1 minute.

❸ Add the beef and stir-fry for another 2–3 minutes until lightly coloured. Stir in the lemon grass and ginger, and remove the wok from the heat.

❹ Remove the beef from the pan or wok and keep to one side. Next, add the peppers and onion to the pan or wok, and stir-fry in the same oil over a high heat for 2–3 minutes until the onions are just turning golden brown and are slightly softened.

❺ Return the beef to the pan, stir in the lime juice, and season to taste with salt and pepper. Serve the stir-fry immediately, while still piping hot, with noodles or rice.

COOK'S TIP
When preparing lemon grass, take care to remove the outer layers, which can be tough and fibrous. Use only the central, tender part, which has the finest flavour.

26

Red-hot Beef with Cashews

INGREDIENTS

500 g/1 lb 2 oz boneless,
  lean beef sirloin,
  sliced thinly
1 tsp vegetable oil

MARINADE
1 tbsp sesame seeds
1 garlic clove, chopped
1 tbsp fresh ginger root,
  chopped finely
1 red bird's-eye chilli,
  chopped
2 tbsp dark soy sauce
1 tsp red curry paste

TO FINISH
1 tsp sesame oil
4 tbsp unsalted
  cashew nuts
1 spring onion, sliced
  thickly on the
  diagonal
cucumber slices,
  to garnish

❶ Cut the beef into 1 cm/½ inch wide strips. Place them in a large, non-metal bowl.

❷ To make the marinade, toast the sesame seeds in a heavy-based pan over a medium heat for 2–3 minutes until golden brown, shaking the pan occasionally.

❸ Place the seeds in a mortar with the garlic, ginger and chilli, and grind with a pestle to a smooth paste. Add the soy sauce and curry paste, and mix well.

❹ Spoon the paste over the beef strips, and toss well to coat the meat evenly. Cover, and leave to marinate in the refrigerator for 2–3 hours, or overnight.

❺ Heat a heavy frying pan or a griddle until it is very hot, and brush with vegetable oil. Place the beef strips on it, and cook quickly, turning often, until lightly browned. Remove from the heat and spoon into a mound on a hot serving dish.

❻ Heat the sesame oil in a small pan and quickly fry the cashew nuts until golden. Take care that they do not burn. Add the spring onion and stir-fry for 30 seconds. Sprinkle the mixture on top of the beef strips and serve the dish immediately, garnished with cucumber slices.

 very easy

serves 4

5 minutes, plus
2–3 hours to
marinate

10 minutes

Pork with Soy Sauce & Sesame Glaze

2 pork fillets, about
275 g/9½ oz each
2 tbsp dark soy sauce
2 tbsp clear honey
2 garlic cloves, crushed
1 tbsp sesame seeds
1 onion, sliced thinly
in rings
1 tbsp seasoned
plain flour
sunflower oil, to fry
crisp salad, to serve

very easy

serves 4

15 minutes

40–45 minutes

❶ Trim any fat from the pork fillets and place them in a wide non-metal dish.

❷ Mix together the soy sauce, honey and garlic. Spread this mixture over the pork fillets, turning the meat to coat it evenly on both sides.

❸ Lift the pork fillets into a roasting tin or a shallow ovenproof dish. Sprinkle the sesame seeds evenly over the meat.

❹ Roast the pork in an oven preheated at 200°C/400°F/ Gas Mark 6 for about 20 minute, spooning any juices over the fillet from time to time. Cover loosely with foil to prevent over-browning, and roast for 10–15 minutes more until the meat is cooked thoroughly.

❺ Meanwhile, dip the onion slices in the flour, and shake off the excess. Heat the oil and fry the onion rings until golden and crisp, turning occasionally. Serve the pork in slices with the fried onions on a bed of crisp salad.

COOK'S TIP
This pork is also excellent served cold, and it is a good choice for picnics, served with a hot chilli relish.

Thai-style Burgers

INGREDIENTS

1 small lemon grass stalk
1 small red chilli,
    deseeded
2 garlic cloves, peeled
2 spring onions
200 g/7 oz closed-cup
    mushrooms
400 g/14 oz minced
    pork
1 tbsp Thai fish sauce
3 tbsp fresh coriander,
    chopped
sunflower oil for
    shallow frying
2 tbsp mayonnaise
1 tbsp lime juice
salt and pepper

TO SERVE
4 sesame hamburger
    buns
shredded Chinese leaves

❶ Place the lemon grass, chilli, garlic and spring onions in a food processor and process to a smooth paste. Add the mushrooms and process until they are very finely chopped.

❷ Add the minced pork, fish sauce and coriander. Season well with salt and pepper, then divide the mixture into 4 equal portions and shape with lightly floured hands into flat burger shapes.

❸ Heat the oil in a frying pan over a medium heat. Add the burgers and fry them for 6–8 minutes, or until they are cooked to your liking.

❹ Meanwhile, mix the mayonnaise with the lime juice. Split the hamburger buns and spread the lime-flavoured mayonnaise on the cut surfaces. Add a few shredded Chinese leaves, top with a burger, and sandwich together. Serve immediately while still hot.

very easy

serves 4

20 minutes

6–8 minutes

Red Lamb Curry

500 g/1 lb 2 oz boneless
   lean leg of lamb
2 tbsp vegetable oil
1 large onion, sliced
2 garlic cloves, crushed
2 tbsp Thai red curry
   paste
150 ml/5 fl oz coconut
   milk
1 tbsp soft light
   brown sugar
1 large red pepper,
   deseeded and sliced
   thickly
120 ml/4 fl oz lamb or
   beef stock
1 tbsp Thai fish sauce
2 tbsp lime juice
227 g/8 oz can water
   chestnuts, drained
2 tbsp fresh coriander,
   chopped
2 tbsp fresh basil,
   chopped
salt and pepper
boiled jasmine rice,
   to serve
fresh basil leaves,
   to garnish

❶ Trim the meat and cut it into 3 cm/1¼ inch cubes. Heat the oil in a large frying pan or a wok over a high heat and stir-fry the onion and garlic for 2–3 minutes until it is softened. Add the meat and fry the mixture quickly until it is lightly and evenly browned.

❷ Stir in the curry paste and cook for a few seconds, then add the coconut milk and sugar, and bring the mixture to the boil. Reduce the heat and simmer for 15 minutes, stirring occasionally.

❸ Stir in the red pepper, stock, fish sauce and lime juice. Cover, and continue simmering for another 15 minutes, or until the meat is tender.

❹ Add the water chestnuts, coriander and basil, and adjust the seasoning to taste. Serve with jasmine rice garnished with fresh basil leaves.

very easy

serves 4

15–20 minutes

30–35 minutes

Chicken & Mango Stir-Fry

6 boneless, skinless chicken thighs
2.5 cm/1 inch piece fresh ginger root, grated
1 garlic clove, crushed
1 small red chilli, deseeded
1 large red pepper
4 spring onions
200 g/7 oz mangetouts
100 g/3½ oz baby corn
1 large, firm, ripe mango
2 tbsp sunflower oil
1 tbsp light soy sauce
3 tbsp rice wine or sherry
1 tsp sesame oil
salt and pepper
sliced chives, to garnish

❶ Cut the chicken into long, thin strips and place in a bowl. Mix together the ginger, garlic and chilli, then stir into the bowl to coat the chicken strips evenly.

❷ Slice the pepper thinly, cutting on the diagonal. Trim the spring onions and slice them on the diagonal. Cut the mangetouts and corn in half on the diagonal. Peel the mango, remove the stone, and slice thinly.

❸ Heat the oil in a large frying pan or a wok over a high heat. Add the chicken and stir-fry for 4–5 minutes until it just turns golden brown. Add the peppers and stir-fry over a medium heat for 4–5 minutes to soften them.

❹ Add the sliced spring onions and the mangetouts and corn, and stir-fry for a minute more.

❺ Mix together the soy sauce, rice wine or sherry, and the sesame oil, and stir into the wok. Add the mango and stir gently for 1 minute to heat thoroughly.

❻ Adjust the seasoning with salt and pepper to taste, and serve immediately. Garnish with chives.

extremely easy

serves 4

15 minutes

10–15 minutes

Thai-spiced Coriander Chicken

INGREDIENTS

4 boneless chicken breasts, without skin
2 garlic cloves, peeled
1 fresh green chilli, deseeded
2 cm/ ¾ inch piece fresh ginger root, peeled
4 tbsp fresh coriander, chopped
rind of 1 lime, grated finely
3 tbsp lime juice
2 tbsp light soy sauce
1 tbsp caster sugar
175 ml/6 fl oz coconut milk
plain boiled rice, to serve
cucumber and radish slices, to garnish

❶ Using a sharp knife, cut 3 deep slashes into the skinned side of each chicken breast. Place the breasts in a single layer in a wide, non-metal dish.

❷ Put the garlic, chilli, ginger, coriander, lime rind and juice, soy sauce, caster sugar and coconut milk in a food processor, and process until a smooth purée forms.

❸ Spread the purée evenly over both sides of the chicken breasts, coating them evenly. Cover the dish, place it in the refrigerator, and leave the chicken breasts to marinate for about 1 hour.

❹ Lift the chicken from the marinade, drain off the excess and place in a grill pan. Grill under a preheated grill for 12–15 minutes until thoroughly and evenly cooked.

❺ Meanwhile, place the remaining marinade in a saucepan and bring to the boil. Lower the heat and simmer for several minutes to heat it thoroughly. Serve it as a sauce with the chicken breasts, accompanied with rice and garnished with cucumber and radish slices.

 very easy

serves 4

15 minutes, plus 1 hour to marinate

15–20 minutes

Duck Breasts with Chilli & Lime

INGREDIENTS

4 boneless duck breasts
2 garlic cloves, crushed
4 tsp light soft brown
    sugar
3 tbsp lime juice
1 tbsp soy sauce
1 tsp chilli sauce
1 tsp vegetable oil
2 tbsp plum jam
125 ml/4 fl oz chicken
    stock
salt and pepper

❶ Using a small, sharp knife, cut deep slashes in the skin of the duck to make a diamond pattern. Place the duck breasts in a wide, non-metal dish.

❷ Mix together the garlic, sugar, lime juice, soy and chilli sauces, then spoon the mixture over the duck breasts, turning well to coat them evenly. Cover the dish with clingfilm and leave to marinate in the refrigerator for at least 3 hours, or preferably overnight.

❸ Drain the duck, reserving the marinade. Heat a large, heavy-based pan until very hot and brush with the oil. Add the duck breasts, skin side down, and cook for about 5 minutes or until the skin is browned and crisp. Tip away the excess fat. Turn the duck breasts over.

❹ Continue cooking on the other side for 2–3 minutes to brown. Add the reserved marinade, plum jam and stock, and simmer for 2 minutes. Adjust the seasoning to taste and serve hot, with the juices spooned over the meat.

 very easy

serves 4

20 minutes, plus 8 hours to marinate

10–15 minutes

COOK'S TIP
To reduce the fat content of this dish, remove the skin from the duck breasts before cooking and reduce the cooking time slightly.

Thai Green Fish Curry

2 tbsp vegetable oil
1 garlic clove, chopped
1 small aubergine, diced
125 g/4 fl oz coconut
   cream
2 tbsp Thai fish sauce
1 tsp sugar
225 g/8 oz firm white fish,
   cut into pieces
125 g/4 fl oz fish stock
2 lime leaves, shredded
   finely
about 15 leaves Thai
   basil, or ordinary basil
plain boiled rice or
   noodles, to serve

GREEN CURRY PASTE
5 fresh green chillies,
   deseeded and chopped
2 tsp chopped lemon grass
1 large shallot, chopped
2 garlic cloves, chopped
1 tsp freshly grated ginger
   or galangal
2 coriander roots,
   chopped
½ tsp ground coriander
¼ tsp ground cumin
1 kaffir lime leaf,
   chopped finely
1 tsp shrimp paste
   (optional)
½ tsp salt

very easy

serves 4

20 minutes

15 minutes

❶ To make the curry paste, put all the ingredients into a blender or a spice grinder and blend them to a smooth paste, adding a little water if necessary. Alternatively, pound the ingredients, using a mortar and pestle, until a smooth paste forms. Set aside.

❷ In a frying pan or a wok, heat the oil until it is almost smoking and add the garlic. Fry until golden. Add the curry paste and stir-fry for a few seconds before adding the aubergine. Stir-fry for 4–5 minutes until softened.

❸ Add the coconut cream. Bring to the boil and stir until the cream thickens and curdles slightly. Add the fish sauce and sugar to the frying pan, and stir well into the mixture.

❹ Add the fish pieces and stock. Simmer for 3–4 minutes, stirring occasionally, until the fish is just tender. Add the lime leaves and basil, and then cook for an additional minute. Remove from the frying pan or serve with plain boiled rice or noodles.

Red Prawn Curry

INGREDIENTS

2 tbsp vegetable oil
1 garlic clove, chopped
  finely
1 tbsp red curry paste
200 ml/7 fl oz coconut
  milk
2 tbsp Thai fish sauce
1 tsp sugar
12 large raw prawns,
  deveined
2 lime leaves, shredded
  finely
1 small red chilli,
  deseeded and
  sliced finely
10 leaves Thai basil, or
  ordinary basil

RED CURRY PASTE
3 dried long red chillies
½ tsp ground coriander
¼ tsp ground cumin
½ tsp ground black
  pepper
2 garlic cloves, chopped
2 lemon grass stalks,
  chopped
1 kaffir lime leaf,
  chopped finely
1 tsp freshly grated
  ginger or galangal
1 tsp shrimp paste
  (optional)
½ tsp salt

very easy

serves 4

15–20 minutes

15–20 minutes

❶ Make the red curry paste. Put all the ingredients in a blender or a spice grinder, and blend to a smooth paste, adding a little water if necessary. A mortar and pestle may also be used. Set aside.

❷ Heat the oil in a wok or a frying pan until it is almost smoking. Add the chopped garlic and fry until golden. Add 1 tablespoon of the curry paste and cook for an additional minute. Add half the coconut milk, the fish sauce, and the sugar. Stir well. The mixture should thicken a little.

❸ Add the prawns and simmer for 3–4 minutes until they turn colour. Add the remaining coconut milk, the lime leaves and the chilli. Cook for an additional 2–3 minutes until the prawns are just tender.

❹ Add the basil leaves to the pan, stir them until they wilt, and serve the curry immediately.

Spicy Coconut Rice with Monkfish & Peas

INGREDIENTS

1 hot red chilli, deseeded
    and chopped
1 tsp crushed chilli flakes
2 garlic cloves, chopped
2 pinches saffron
3 tbsp chopped coarsely
    mint leaves
4 tbsp olive oil
2 tbsp lemon juice
375 g / 12 oz monkfish
    fillet, cut into bite-
    sized pieces
1 onion, chopped finely
225 g / 8 oz long grain
    rice
400 g / 14 oz canned
    chopped tomatoes
200 ml / 7 fl oz coconut
    milk
115 g / 4 oz peas
salt and pepper
2 tbsp chopped
    coriander, to garnish

❶ In a food processor or a blender, blend together the fresh and dried chilli, garlic, saffron, mint, olive oil, and lemon juice until chopped finely but not smooth.

❷ Put the monkfish into a non-metal dish and pour over the spice paste, mixing together well. Set aside for 20 minutes to marinate.

❸ Heat a large saucepan until very hot. Using a slotted spoon, lift the monkfish from the marinade and add in batches to the hot pan. Cook for 3–4 minutes until browned and firm. Remove with a slotted spoon and set aside.

❹ Add the onion and remaining marinade to the same pan and cook for 5 minutes until softened and lightly browned. Add the rice and stir until well coated. Add the tomatoes and coconut milk. Bring to a boil, cover, and simmer very gently for 15 minutes. Stir in the peas, season, and arrange the fish over the top. Cover with foil and continue to cook over a very low heat for 5 minutes. Serve garnished with the chopped coriander.

very easy

serves 4

10–15 minutes,
plus 20 minutes
to marinate

35 minutes

Steamed Yellow Fish Fillets

INGREDIENTS

500 g/1 lb 2 oz firm fish
  fillets, such as red
  snapper, sole or
  monkfish
1 dried red bird's eye
  chilli
1 small onion, chopped
3 garlic cloves, chopped
2 sprigs fresh coriander
1 tsp coriander seeds
½ tsp turmeric
½ tsp ground black
  pepper
1 tbsp Thai fish sauce
2 tbsp coconut milk
1 small egg, beaten
2 tbsp rice flour
red and green chilli
  strips, to garnish
soy sauce, to serve

very easy

serves 4

15–20 minutes

10–15 minutes

❶ Remove any skin from the fish and cut the fillets on the diagonal into long 2 cm/¾ inch wide strips.

❷ Place the dried chilli, onion, garlic, coriander and coriander seeds in a mortar and grind with a pestle to a smooth paste.

❸ Add the turmeric, pepper, fish sauce, coconut milk and beaten egg, stirring well to mix evenly.

❹ Dip the fish strips into the paste mixture, then into the rice flour to coat lightly.

❺ Bring the water in the bottom of a steamer to the boil, then arrange the fish strips in the top part of the steamer. Cover and steam the fish strips for about 12–15 minutes until they are just firm.

❻ Garnish the fish with chilli strips and serve with soy sauce and an accompaniment of stir-fried vegetables.

COOK'S TIP

If you do not have a steamer, improvise by placing a large metal colander over a large pan of boiling water and cover with an upturned plate to enclose the fish as it steams.

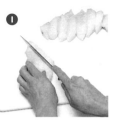

Baked Fish with Pepper, Chillies & Basil

very easy

serves 4

10–15 minutes

40–45 minutes

COOK'S TIP
Large red chillies are
less hot than the tiny
red bird's-eye chillies,
so you can use them
more freely in cooked
dishes such as this
for a mild heat. If you
prefer a milder dish,
remove the seeds.

❶ Reserve a few fresh basil leaves for the garnish, and tuck the rest inside the body cavity of the fish.

❷ Heat 1 tablespoon oil in a wide frying pan and fry the fish quickly to brown, turning once. Place the fish on a large piece of foil in a roasting tin and spoon the fish sauce over the fish. Wrap the fish loosely in the foil and bake in an oven preheated to 190°C/375°F/Gas Mark 5 for 25–30 minutes until just cooked though.

❸ Meanwhile, heat the remaining oil and fry the garlic, galangal and chillies for 30 seconds. Add the pepper and stir-fry for another 2–3 minutes to soften.

❹ Stir in the sugar, rice vinegar and water, then add the tomatoes and bring the sauce to the boil. Remove the pan from the heat.

❺ Remove the fish from the oven and transfer to a warmed serving plate. Add the fish juices to the pan, then spoon the sauce over the fish and scatter the tomatoes and reserved basil leaves over it. Serve the dish immediately.

Spiced Tuna in Sweet & Sour Sauce

INGREDIENTS

4 fresh tuna steaks,
   about 500 g/1 lb 2 oz
   total weight
¼ tsp ground black
   pepper
2 tbsp groundnut oil
1 onion, diced
1 garlic clove, crushed
½ cucumber, deseeded
   and cut into
   matchsticks
2 pineapple slices, diced
1 tsp fresh ginger root,
   chopped finely
1 tbsp soft light brown
   sugar
1 tbsp cornflour
1½ tbsp lime juice
1 tbsp Thai fish sauce
250 ml/9 fl oz fish stock
cucumber slices,
   to garnish

❶ Sprinkle the tuna steaks with pepper on both sides. Heat a heavy frying pan or a griddle, and brush with a little of the oil. Arrange the tuna on the griddle and cook for about 8 minutes, turning them over once.

❷ Heat the remaining oil in another pan and fry the onion and garlic gently for 3–4 minutes to soften.

❸ Remove from the heat and stir in the cucumber, pineapple, ginger and sugar.

❹ Blend the cornflour with the lime juice and fish sauce, then stir into the stock and add to the pan. Stir over a medium heat until boiling, then cook for 1–2 minutes until thickened and clear.

❺ Spoon the sauce over the tuna and serve garnished with cucumber slices.

extremely easy

serves 4

10 minutes

15–20 minutes

Thai-spiced Salmon

INGREDIENTS

2.5 cm/1 in piece fresh
root ginger, grated
1 tsp coriander seeds,
crushed
¼ tsp chilli powder
1 tbsp lime juice
1 tsp sesame oil
4 pieces salmon fillet
with skin, about
150 g/5½ oz each
2 tbsp vegetable oil
boiled rice and stir-fried
vegetables, to serve

❶ Mix together the grated ginger, crushed coriander, chilli powder, lime juice and sesame oil.

❷ Place the salmon on a wide, non-metal plate or dish and spoon the mixture over the flesh side of the fillets, spreading it to coat each piece of salmon evenly.

❸ Cover the dish with clingfilm and chill the salmon in the refrigerator for 30 minutes.

❹ Heat a wide, heavy-based frying pan or a griddle pan with the oil over a high heat. Place the salmon on the hot pan or griddle, skin side down.

❺ Cook the salmon for 4–5 minutes, without turning, until the salmon is crusty underneath and the flesh flakes easily. Serve at once with the boiled rice and stir-fried vegetables.

 extremely easy

serves 4

10 minutes, plus 30 minutes to chill

5 minutes

COOK'S TIP

It is important to use a heavy-based pan or solid griddle, so the fish cooks evenly without sticking. If the fish is very thick, turn it over carefully to cook on the other side for 2–3 minutes.

Spicy Scallops with Lime & Chilli

❶ Trim the scallops to remove any black intestine, then wash and pat dry. Separate the corals from the white parts, then slice each white part in half horizontally, making 2 rounds.

❷ Heat the butter and oil in a frying pan or a wok. Add the garlic and ginger and stir-fry for 1 minute without browning. Add the spring onions and stir-fry for another minute.

❸ Add the scallops to the frying pan and continue stir-frying over a high heat for 4–5 minutes. Stir in the lime rind, chilli and lime juice and cook the mixture gently for another minute.

❹ Serve the scallops hot, with the juices spooned over them, garnished with lime wedges and accompanied by boiled rice.

extremely easy

serves 4

15 minutes

7–8 minutes

Light Meals & Salads

Thai salads are packed with unusual ingredients. Thai Noodle Salad with Prawns has a base of thin rice noodles tossed in a zesty lime-juice dressing with fresh green mangetouts and pink prawns. This salad is topped with chopped peanuts, a typical Thai garnish. For an elegant dish to include in a buffet lunch, try Sweet & Sour Seafood Salad, with mussels, scallops, squid and prawns. Thai omelettes are luxurious creations. The Crab Omelette on page 62 is bursting with its spiced crabmeat stuffing.

Thai Noodle Salad with Prawns

INGREDIENTS

*80 g/3 oz rice vermicelli
or rice sticks*
*175 g/6 oz mangetouts,
cut crossways in half,
if large*
5 tbsp lime juice
4 tbsp Thai fish sauce
1 tbsp sugar, or to taste
*2.5 cm/1 inch piece fresh
ginger root, peeled
and chopped finely*
*1 fresh red chilli,
deseeded and sliced
thinly on the diagonal*
*4 tbsp chopped fresh
coriander or mint, plus
extra for garnishing*
*10 cm/4 inch piece of
cucumber, peeled,
deseeded and diced*
*2 spring onions, sliced
thinly on the diagonal*
*16–20 large cooked,
peeled prawns*
*2 tbsp chopped unsalted
peanuts or cashews
(optional)*
*4 whole cooked prawns
and lemon slices, to
garnish*

❶ Put the rice noodles in a large bowl and pour in enough hot water to cover them. Leave them to stand for about 4 minutes until soft. Drain and rinse under cold running water, drain again, and set aside.

❷ Bring a saucepan of water to the boil. Add the mangetouts and return to the boil. Simmer for 1 minute. Drain, rinse under cold running water until cold, then drain again, and set aside.

❸ In a large bowl, whisk together the lime juice, fish sauce, sugar, ginger, chilli and coriander. Stir the cucumber and spring onions into the mixture. Add the drained noodles, the mangetouts and the prawns. Toss the salad gently together until the ingredients are coated with the sauce.

❹ Divide the noodle salad among 4 large plates. Sprinkle with chopped coriander and the peanuts (if using), then garnish each plate with a whole prawn and a lemon slice. Serve immediately.

extremely easy

serves 4

10–15 minutes,
plus 4 minutes
to stand

5 minutes

Thai Crab Omelette

225 g/8 oz white crab
meat, fresh, or thawed
if frozen
3 spring onions,
chopped finely
1 tbsp chopped fresh
coriander
1 tbsp chopped fresh
chives
pinch cayenne pepper
1 tbsp vegetable oil,
for cooking
2 garlic cloves, crushed
1 tsp freshly grated
ginger root
1 red chilli, deseeded and
chopped finely
2 tbsp lime juice
2 lime leaves, shredded
2 tsp sugar
2 tsp Thai fish sauce
3 eggs, beaten lightly
4 tbsp coconut cream
1 tsp salt
1 tbsp vegetable oil
spring onion slivers,
to garnish

❶ Put the crab meat into a bowl and check for any small pieces of shell. Add the spring onions, coriander, chives, and cayenne pepper, and set aside.

❷ Heat 1 tablespoon of vegetable oil in a pan, add the garlic, ginger and chilli, and stir-fry for 30 seconds. Add the lime juice, lime leaves, sugar and fish sauce. Simmer for 3–4 minutes until reduced. Remove from the heat and allow to cool. Add to the crab mixture and set aside.

❸ Beat the eggs lightly with the coconut cream and salt. In a frying pan, heat the remaining vegetable oil over a medium heat. Add the egg mixture, and as it sets on the bottom, carefully pull the edges in toward the centre, allowing unset egg to run underneath.

❹ When the egg is nearly set, spoon the crab mixture down the centre. Cook for an additional 1–2 minutes to finish setting the egg, then turn the omelette out of the pan onto a serving dish. Allow to cool, then refrigerate for 2–3 hours, or overnight. Cut into 4 pieces and garnish with spring onion slivers.

very easy

serves 4

10 minutes, plus
8 hours to chill

8 minutes

Thai Seafood Salad

INGREDIENTS

450 g/1 lb live mussels
8 raw tiger prawns
350 g/12 oz squid,
    cleaned and sliced
    widthways into rings
115 g/4 oz cooked
    peeled prawns
½ red onion, sliced finely
½ red pepper, deseeded
    and sliced finely
115 g/4 oz beansprouts
115 g/14 oz shredded
    pak choi

DRESSING
1 garlic clove, crushed
1 tsp grated fresh
    ginger root
1 red chilli, deseeded and
    chopped finely
2 tbsp chopped fresh
    coriander
1 tbsp lime juice
1 tsp finely grated lime
    rind
1 tbsp light soy sauce
5 tbsp sunflower or
    groundnut oil
2 tsp sesame oil
salt and pepper
4 tbsp cold water

❶ Scrub or scrape the mussel shells and remove any beards. Place in a large saucepan with just the water that clings to their shells. Cook over a high heat for 3–4 minutes, shaking the pan occasionally, until all the mussels have opened. Discard any that remain closed. Strain the mussels, reserve the poaching liquid, and refresh the mussels under cold water. Drain again and set aside.

❷ Bring the reserved poaching liquid to a boil and add the tiger prawns. Simmer for 5 minutes. Add the squid and simmer for 2 minutes. Remove the seafood with a slotted spoon and plunge into cold water. Reserve the poaching liquid. Drain the prawns and squid again.

❸ Remove the mussels from their shells and put into a bowl with the prawns and squid. Chill for 1 hour.

❹ For the dressing, put all the ingredients except the oils into a blender, and blend to a smooth paste. Add the oils, poaching liquid, seasoning and water, and blend again.

❺ Combine the onion, pepper, beansprouts, and pak choi in a bowl and toss with 3 tablespoons of dressing. Transfer to a serving plate. Toss the remaining dressing with the seafood to coat, and add to the vegetables. Serve at once.

very easy

serves 4

20 minutes, plus
1 hour to chill

10–15 minutes

Fish Cakes with Hot Peanut Dip

INGREDIENTS

350 g/12 oz white fish
   fillet without skin,
   such as cod or
   haddock
1 tbsp Thai fish sauce
2 tsp Thai red curry paste
1 tbsp lime juice
1 garlic clove, crushed
4 dried kaffir lime leaves,
   crumbled
1 egg white
3 tbsp fresh coriander,
   chopped
salt and pepper
vegetable oil for
   shallow frying
green salad leaves,
   to serve

PEANUT DIP
1 small red chilli
1 tbsp light soy sauce
1 tbsp lime juice
1 tbsp soft light
   brown sugar
3 tbsp chunky
   peanut butter
4 tbsp coconut milk

❶ Put the fish fillet in a food processor with the fish sauce, curry paste, lime juice, garlic, lime leaves and egg white, and process until a smooth paste forms.

❷ Stir in the fresh coriander and quickly process again until mixed. Divide the mixture into 8–10 pieces and roll them into balls, then flatten the balls to make round patties. Set the patties aside.

❸ To make the dip, halve and deseed the chilli, then chop finely. Place in a small pan with the remaining ingredients for the dip and heat gently, stirring constantly, until well blended. Adjust the seasoning to taste.

❹ Shallow-fry the fish cakes in batches for 3–4 minutes on each side until golden brown. Drain on kitchen paper and serve the fish cakes hot on a bed of green salad leaves accompanied by the chilli-flavoured peanut dip.

very easy

serves 4–5

10 minutes

10–20 minutes

Thai Stir-fried Chicken with Vegetables

INGREDIENTS

3 tbsp sesame oil
350 g/12 oz chicken
    breast, sliced thinly
2 shallots, sliced
2 garlic cloves,
    chopped finely
2.5 cm/1 inch piece fresh
    root ginger, grated
1 green chilli,
    chopped finely
3 courgettes, sliced thinly
1 each red and green
    pepper, sliced thinly
2 tbsp ground almonds
1 tbsp oyster sauce
1 tsp ground cinnamon
50 g/1¾ oz creamed
    coconut, grated
salt and pepper

❶ Heat the sesame oil in a wok, add the chicken, season with salt and pepper, and stir-fry for about 4 minutes.

❷ Add the shallots, garlic, ginger and chilli, and stir-fry for 2 minutes.

❸ Add the courgettes and peppers, and cook for about 1 minute.

❹ Add the almonds, oyster sauce, cinnamon, coconut and season to taste. Stir-fry for 1 minute and serve.

very easy

serves 4

10–15 minutes

10 minutes

COOK'S TIP

Creamed coconut is sold in blocks in supermarkets and Asian stores. It is a useful storecupboard standby as it adds richness and depth of flavour.

Thai-style Open Crabmeat Sandwich

❶ Mix half the lime juice with the ginger and lemon grass. Add the mayonnaise and mix well.

❷ Spread 1 tablespoon of mayonnaise smoothly over each slice of bread.

❸ Halve the avocado and remove the stone. Peel and slice the flesh thinly, then arrange the slices on the bread. Sprinkle with lime juice.

❹ Spoon the crab meat over the avocado, then add any remaining lime juice. Spoon the remaining mayonnaise over the sandwiches, and season with freshly ground black pepper. Top with a sprig of coriander, and serve immediately.

 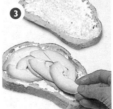 

extremely easy

serves 2

5–10 minutes

0 minutes

COOK'S TIP

To make lime and ginger mayonnaise, put 2 egg yolks, 1 tablespoon lime juice and ½ teaspoon grated ginger root in a blender. With the motor running, add 300 ml/10 fl oz olive oil, drop by drop, until thick and smooth. Add seasoning.

Steamed Mussels with Lemon Grass & Basil

INGREDIENTS

1 kg/2 lb 4 oz fresh
   mussels in shells
2 shallots, chopped
   finely
1 lemon grass stalk,
   sliced finely
1 garlic clove, chopped
   finely
3 tbsp rice wine or sherry
2 tbsp lime juice
1 tbsp Thai fish sauce
25 g/1 oz butter
4 tbsp fresh basil,
   chopped
salt and pepper
fresh basil leaves, to
   garnish
crusty bread, to serve

extremely easy

serves 4

15–20 minutes

10 minutes

❶ Clean the mussels, removing any beards and dirt. Rinse in clear water and drain. Discard any that do not close when tapped, or have damaged shells.

❷ Place the shallots, lemon grass, garlic, rice wine, lime juice and fish sauce in a large pan and place over a high heat.

❸ Add the mussels, cover with a lid, and steam the mussels for 2–3 minutes, shaking the pan occasionally during cooking until the mussel shells open.

❹ Discard any mussels which have not opened, then stir in the chopped basil and season with salt and pepper.

❺ Scoop out the mussels with a perforated spoon and divide between 4 deep bowls. Quickly whisk the butter into the pan juices, then pour the juices over the mussels.

❻ Garnish each bowl with fresh basil leaves and serve with plenty of crusty bread to mop up the juices.

COOK'S TIP
If you prefer to serve this dish as a main course, this amount will be enough for two portions. Fresh clams in shells are also very good when cooked by this method.

Lemon Grass Chicken Skewers

INGREDIENTS

2 long or 4 short lemon
   grass stalks
2 large boneless,
   skinless chicken
   breasts, about
   400 g/14 oz in total
1 small egg white
1 carrot, grated finely
1 small red chilli,
   deseeded and
   chopped
2 tbsp fresh garlic chives,
   chopped
2 tbsp fresh coriander,
   chopped
1 tbsp sunflower oil
salt and pepper
coriander and lime slices,
   to garnish

very easy

serves 4

25 minutes,
plus 15 minutes
to chill

4–6 minutes

❶ If the lemon grass stalks are long, cut them in half across the middle to make 4 short lengths. Cut each stalk in half lengthways, so you have 8 sticks.

❷ Chop the chicken pieces coarsely and place them in a food processor with the egg white. Process to a smooth paste, then add the carrot, chilli, chives, coriander and salt and pepper. Process for a few seconds to mix well.

❸ Chill the mixture in the refrigerator for about 15 minutes. Divide the mixture into 8 equal portions, and use your hands to shape the mixture around the skewers made from lemon grass.

❹ Brush the skewers with oil and grill under a preheated medium–hot grill for 4–6 minutes, turning them occasionally, until golden brown and cooked thoroughly. Alternatively, barbecue over medium–hot coals.

❺ Serve hot, and garnish with coriander and slices of lime.

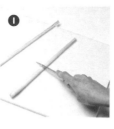

COOK'S TIP

If whole lemon grass
stalks are not available,
use wooden or bamboo
skewers instead, and
add ¼ teaspoon ground
lemon grass to the
mixture with the other
flavourings.

Sweet & Sour Seafood Salad

INGREDIENTS

18 fresh mussels in shells
6 large scallops
200 g / 7 oz baby squid,
    cleaned
2 shallots, chopped
    finely
6 raw tiger prawns,
    peeled and deveined
¼ cucumber
1 carrot, peeled
¼ head Chinese leaves,
    shredded

DRESSING
4 tbsp lime juice
2 garlic cloves, chopped
    finely
2 tbsp Thai fish sauce
1 tsp sesame oil
1 tbsp soft light brown
    sugar
2 tbsp fresh mint,
    chopped
¼ tsp ground black
    pepper
salt

❶ Clean the mussels, discarding any damaged or open ones that do not close when firmly tapped. Steam them in just the water which clings to them for 1–2 minutes until opened. Lift out with a perforated spoon, reserving the liquid in the pan. Discard any unopened mussels.

❷ Separate the corals from the scallops and cut the whites in half horizontally. Cut the tentacles from the squid and slice the body cavities into rings.

❸ Add the shallots to the liquid in the pan and simmer over a high heat until the liquid is reduced to about 3 tablespoons. Add the scallops, squid and tiger prawns, and stir for 2–3 minutes until cooked. Remove from the heat and spoon the mixture into a wide bowl.

❹ Cut the cucumber and carrot in half lengthways, then slice thinly on the diagonal to make long, pointed slices. Toss with the Chinese leaves.

❺ To make the dressing, place all the ingredients in a screw-top jar and shake well until they are evenly combined. Season with salt.

❻ Toss the vegetables and seafood gently, then spoon the dressing over them, and serve immediately.

very easy

serves 4–6

10–15 minutes

10 minutes

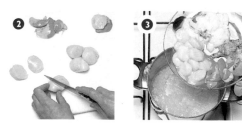

Warm Salad of Tuna & Tomatoes with Ginger Dressing

INGREDIENTS

50 g/1¾ oz Chinese
    leaves, shredded
3 tbsp rice wine
2 tbsp Thai fish sauce
1 tbsp fresh ginger root,
    shredded finely
1 garlic clove,
    chopped finely
½ small red bird's eye
    chilli, chopped finely
2 tsp soft light brown
    sugar
2 tbsp lime juice
400 g/14 oz tuna steak
sunflower oil, for
    brushing
125 g/4½ oz cherry
    tomatoes
fresh mint leaves and
    sprigs, to garnish

❶ Place a small pile of shredded Chinese leaves on a serving plate. Place the rice wine, fish sauce, ginger, garlic, chilli, brown sugar and 1 tablespoon of lime juice in a screw-top jar, and shake well to combine evenly.

❷ Cut the tuna into strips of an even thickness. Sprinkle with the remaining lime juice.

❸ Brush a wide frying pan or a griddle with the oil, and heat until very hot. Arrange the tuna strips in the pan and cook until just firm and light golden, turning them over once. Remove and set aside.

❹ Add the tomatoes to the pan and cook over a high heat until lightly browned. Spoon the tuna and tomatoes over the Chinese leaves, and spoon the dressing over the top. Garnish with fresh mint and serve warm.

extremely easy

serves 4

20 minutes

10–15 minutes

Hot & Sour Noodles

INGREDIENTS

250 g/9 oz dried medium
   egg noodles
1 tbsp sesame oil
1 tbsp chilli oil
1 garlic clove, crushed
2 spring onions,
   chopped finely
55 g/2 oz button
   mushrooms, sliced
40 g/½ oz dried Chinese
   black mushrooms,
   soaked and sliced
2 tbsp lime juice
3 tbsp light soy sauce
1 tsp sugar

TO SERVE
shredded Chinese leaves
2 tbsp coriander
2 tbsp toasted peanuts

extremely easy

serves 4

10 minutes

10–15 minutes

❶ Cook the noodles in a large pan of boiling water for 3–4 minutes, or according to the package directions. Drain well, return to the pan, toss with the sesame oil, and set aside.

❷ Heat the chilli oil in a large frying pan or a wok, and quickly stir-fry the garlic, spring onions and button mushrooms to soften them.

❸ Add the black mushrooms, lime juice, soy sauce and sugar, and continue stir-frying until the mixture is boiling. Add the noodles and toss to mix.

❹ Spoon the noodles over the Chinese leaves and serve sprinkled with shredded coriander and chopped peanuts.

COOK'S TIP
Thai chilli oil is very hot, so if you want a milder flavour, use vegetable oil to cook, then add a dribble of chilli oil for seasoning.

Desserts

The Thai make refreshing use of classic ingredients, such as lime juice and coconut milk, in their desserts. The rind and the juice of a lime are used in Pineapple with Cardamom & Lime, a cool dessert to make a perfect end to a spicy Thai meal. Coconut milk adds a special flavour to custard. Coconut Custard Squares are a variation on the classic baked egg custard, served warm, while Mangoes in Lemon Grass Syrup is a chilled dessert for hot days and warm evenings.

Mangoes in Lemon Grass Syrup

INGREDIENTS

2 large, ripe mangoes
1 lime
1 lemon grass stalk,
   chopped
3 tbsp caster sugar

❶ Halve the mangoes, remove the stones, and peel the skins carefully from the flesh.

❷ Slice the flesh into long, thin slices and gently arrange them in a wide serving dish.

❸ Remove a few shreds of the rind from the lime with a sharp knife, and reserve them to use for decoration, then cut the lime in half and squeeze out the juice.

❹ Place the lime juice in a small pan with the lemon grass and sugar. Heat gently without boiling until the sugar is completely dissolved. Remove from the heat and allow to cool completely.

❺ Strain the cooled syrup into a jug and pour evenly over the mango slices.

❻ Scatter with the lime rind strips, cover and chill before serving. Serve chilled.

 extremely easy

serves 4

15 minutes, plus
1 hour to chill

5 minutes

COOK'S TIP
To serve this dessert on a hot day, particularly if it is to stand for a while, place the dish on a bed of crushed ice to keep the fruit and syrup chilled.

Pineapple with Cardamom & Lime

1 pineapple
2 cardamom pods
1 strip lime rind,
*   pared thinly*
1 tbsp soft light brown
*   sugar*
3 tbsp lime juice
mint sprigs and whipped
*   cream, to decorate*

❶ Cut the top and base from the pineapple, cut away the peel and remove the 'eyes' from the flesh. Cut into quarters and remove the core. Slice the pineapple lengthways.

❷ Put the seeds from the cardamom pods in a mortar, crush them with a pestle, and place them in a pan with the lime rind and 4 tablespoons of water. Heat until the mixture is boiling, then simmer for 30 seconds.

❸ Remove from the heat and add the sugar, then cover and leave to infuse for 5 minutes.

❹ Stir to dissolve the sugar completely, add the lime juice, then strain the syrup over the pineapple. Chill for about 30 minutes.

❺ Arrange the pineapple on a serving dish, spoon the syrup over the top, and decorate the dessert with mint sprigs and whipped cream before serving.

very easy

serves 4

10–15 minutes, plus 35 minutes to infuse and chill

5 minutes

COOK'S TIP
To remove the eyes from pineapple, cut off the peel, and cut a V-shaped downward channel with a small, sharp knife. Cut diagonally through the lines of brown eyes, to make spiralling cuts around the fruit.

Coconut Custard Squares

1 tsp butter, melted
6 medium eggs
400 ml/14 fl oz coconut
  milk
175 g/6 oz soft light
  brown sugar
pinch of salt
shreds of coconut and
  lime rind, to decorate

❶ Brush the butter over the inside of a 19 cm/7½ inch square buttered ovenproof dish or tin, about 4 cm/1½ inch in depth.

❷ Beat the eggs in a large bowl and beat in the coconut milk, sugar and salt.

❸ Place the bowl over a pan of gently simmering water and stir with a wooden spoon for 15 minutes, or until it begins to thicken. Pour into the prepared dish or tin.

❹ Bake the custard in an oven preheated at 180°C/350°F/Gas Mark 4 for 20–25 minutes until just set. Remove from the oven and allow to cool completely.

❺ Turn the custard out of the dish or pan and cut the custard into squares. Serve decorated with coconut shreds, strips of lime rind and slices of fruit.

 easy

serves 4

5 minutes

40–45 minutes

  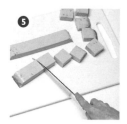

COOK'S TIP
Keep an eye on the custard as it bakes, because the texture will spoil if it overcooks. When it comes out of the oven, it should be barely set and slightly wobbly in the centre. It firms slightly as it cools.

Banana Fritters in Coconut Batter

INGREDIENTS

70 g / 2½ oz plain flour
2 tbsp rice flour
1 tbsp caster sugar
1 egg, separated
150 ml/5 fl oz coconut
    milk
4 large bananas
sunflower oil for
    deep frying

TO DECORATE
1 tsp icing sugar
1 tsp ground cinnamon
lime wedges

very easy

serves 4

8–10 minutes

5–8 minutes

COOK'S TIP
If you can buy the baby
finger bananas that are
popular in this dish in
the East, leave them
whole for coating and
frying.

❶ Sift the plain flour, rice flour and sugar into a bowl and make a well in the centre. Add the egg yolk and coconut milk.

❷ Beat the mixture until a smooth, thick batter forms. Whisk the egg white in a clean, dry bowl until stiff enough to hold soft peaks. Fold it into the batter lightly and evenly.

❸ Heat a 6 cm/2½ inch depth of oil in a large pan to 180°C/ 350°F, or until a cube of bread browns in 30 seconds. Cut the bananas in half crossways, then dip them quickly into the batter to coat them.

❹ Drop the bananas carefully into the hot oil and fry in batches for 2–3 minutes until golden brown, turning once.

❺ Drain on paper towels. Sprinkle with icing sugar and cinnamon, and serve immediately, with lime wedges for squeezing juice as desired.

 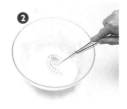 

Thai Rice Pudding

100 g/3½ oz short-grain rice
2 tbsp palm sugar
1 cardamom pod, split
300 ml/10 fl oz coconut milk
150 ml/5 fl oz water
3 eggs
200 ml/7 fl oz coconut cream
1½ tbsp caster sugar
fresh fruit, to serve
sweetened coconut flakes, to decorate

easy

serves 4

20 minutes

1 hour
30 minutes

COOK'S TIP
Cardamom is a powerful spice, so if you find it too strong it can be left out altogether, or replaced with a little ground cinnamon.

❶ Place the rice and palm sugar in a pan. Put the seeds from the cardamom pod in a mortar, crush them with a pestle and add to the pan. Stir in the coconut milk and water.

❷ Bring the mixture to the boil, stirring to dissolve the sugar. Lower the heat and simmer, uncovered, stirring occasionally for about 20 minutes until the rice is tender and most of the liquid is absorbed.

❸ Spoon the rice into 4 individual ovenproof dishes and spread evenly. Place the dishes in a wide roasting tin and fill with water to reach about halfway up the sides of the dishes.

❹ Beat together the eggs, coconut cream and caster sugar and spoon the mixture over the rice. Cover with foil and bake in a preheated oven to 180°C/350°F/Gas Mark 4 for 45–50 minutes until the custard sets.

❺ Serve the rice puddings warm or cold, decorated with coconut flakes, and accompanied by fresh fruit.

Steamed Coconut Cake with Lime & Ginger Syrup

INGREDIENTS

2 large eggs, separated
pinch of salt
100 g/3½ oz caster sugar
75 g/2¾ oz butter,
    melted and cooled
5 tbsp coconut milk
150 g/5½ oz self-raising
    flour
½ tsp baking powder
3 tbsp desiccated
    coconut
4 tbsp stem ginger syrup
3 tbsp lime juice

TO DECORATE
3 pieces stem ginger,
    diced
curls of fresh coconut,
    grated
lime rind, grated finely

❶ Cut a 28 cm/11 inch round of non-stick paper and press into an 18 cm/7 inch steamer basket to line it.

❷ Whisk the egg whites with the salt until stiff. Gradually whisk in the sugar, 1 tablespoon at a time, whisking hard after each addition, until the mixture stands in stiff peaks.

❸ Whisk in the yolks, then quickly stir in the butter and coconut milk. Sift the flour and baking powder over the mixture, then fold in lightly and evenly with a large metal spoon. Fold in the coconut.

❹ Spoon the mixture into the lined steamer basket and tuck the spare paper over the top. Place the basket over boiling water, cover, and steam for 30 minutes.

❺ Turn out the cake onto a plate, remove the paper, and cool slightly. Mix together the ginger syrup and lime juice, and spoon over the cake. Cut into squares and decorate with diced preserved stem ginger, curls of fresh coconut, and lime rind.

easy

serves 8

15 minutes

30 minutes